BEAT HEAT EAT

GENTLEMEN...RAISE YOUR FORKS

BEAT HEAT EAT

COOKING MANUAL

EAT OR DIE

DEAN LAHN

Wakefield
Press

Wakefield Press
1 The Parade West
Kent Town
South Australia 5067
www.wakefieldpress.com.au

First published 2009
Copyright © Dean Lahn, 2009

Printed and bound by
Hyde Park Press, Adelaide

National Library of Australia
Cataloguing-in-Publication entry

Author: Lahn, Dean.
Title: Beat heat eat/Dean Lahn.
ISBN: 978 1 86254 758 2 (pbk.).
Subjects: Cookery.
                 Quick and easy cookery.
Dewey Number: 641.512

GET IT HERE

SAVE MANKIND. POST YOUR MODS AND
RECIPES AT www.BeatHeatEat.com

INTRO

Yeah.

I'll be the first to admit that some, most, of these recipes need a little time to get your head around. That's okay. It's just you've never heard someone say it's okay to ram a beer can up a chicken's clacker, or simmer your dinner in Coke. Relax. Leave the cooking to the experts. Here you're just going to fix something to eat and kick back. Nobody's going to judge you. It's just you, me, and the chicken.

WARNING

If you don't eat you will die

But you don't cook, right? Great. This book isn't a cookbook. It's a manual that shows you how to heat food so you don't starve.

Treat this book as a guide

We're standing at the edge of some very rough territory here. So rough in fact some people will be shocked you ever dared go there. But that's why grazing and trailblazing is exciting.

The ingredients and quantities suggested in this book are just that – suggestions. If you like something, add a bit more. If you don't like it, cut it out.

Be aware

Oven temperatures will be different. Microwave times and temperatures will vary. The times specified in the recipes work in my kitchen. They might be different in yours. Don't forget to check your work while it's cooking. If you can get something warm and edible on the plate, you win.

On every page there are diagrams to assist you in your prep as well as room to write any notes and mods you may find. If they work for you they'll work for others. Go to to www.beatheateat.com and submit your findings. The best suggestions will get posted and you'll be almost famous.

Some things I found out along the way ...

Ease up, Turbo. Not everything is cooked on flat-out high. In fact once you get the thing hot it's almost always a case of dialling the heat back down and just cruising home.

The Golden Rule of chicken cooking is 'If it's all white, it's all right'.

It's okay to make a mess when you're cooking. Just as long as everything is tidy by the time She comes in, you're sweet.

[QWIK FIXES]

1

Have you ever come in late and felt the need for a melted cheese toastie? Quickly satisfy your craving with this trick.

YOU WILL NEED:
(A) a toaster
(B) bread
(C) cheese

DIAGRAM 1

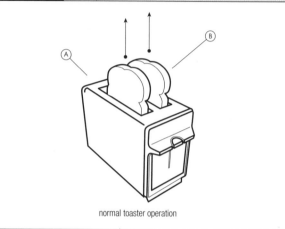

normal toaster operation

DIAGRAM 2

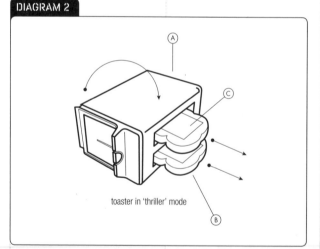

toaster in 'thriller' mode

HOW IT'S DONE:

Grab your toaster and turn it into a grilling machine by flipping it onto its side.

Work to the height of the slots in the toaster. Press the toppings flat if you're over the limit.

Insert bread and cheese into toaster, ensuring the heat elements are clear of the toppings.

Heat until done or the toaster pops.

Keep a close eye on the toaster and be ready to hit the eject button. This kid can light up real quick.

WARNING:
Use this shortcut at your own risk. You may also want to check the warranty on your toaster.

NOTES / MODS

So, you've gone to the trouble of making plunger coffee. Notice how there's always some left? Don't waste it. Do the following and you won't have to go to all that trouble again.

YOU WILL NEED:

(A) left-over plunger coffee

(B) 1 ice-cube tray

(C) 1 mug

DIAGRAM 1

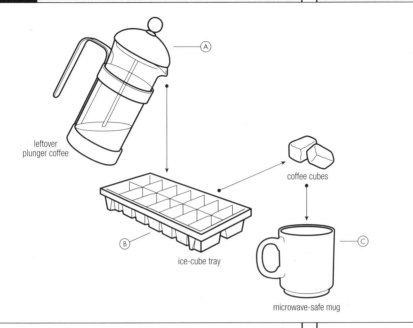

Ⓐ

leftover plunger coffee

coffee cubes

Ⓑ

ice-cube tray

Ⓒ

microwave-safe mug

HOW IT'S DONE:

Pour any left-over coffee into an ice-cube tray. The next time you want a cup of coffee, break out a couple of cubes into a microwave-safe mug. Nuke them until they're melted and warmed through. Drink.

If you're into flavoured coffees, this is a great way to make the most of your resources.

INSTANT COFFEE

THE STEAK OUT

You're standing over a grill with a dozen steaks on the go – everybody wants theirs done differently. Armed with the knowledge that meat tissue tightens when it's heated, give this a try.

YOU WILL NEED:
(A) 2 hands
(preferably yours)

DIAGRAM 1

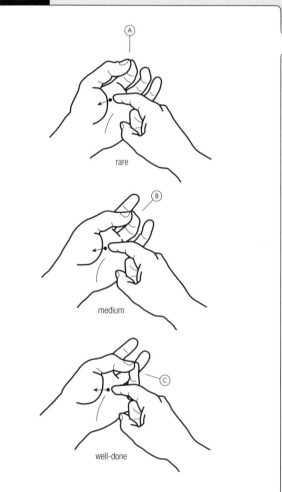

rare

medium

well-done

HOW IT'S DONE:

Rare (A)
Touch your thumb with your pointer finger and gently push the fleshy part of your hand at the base of your thumb. Now push the steak. When they feel similar whip it off the grill and serve.

Medium (B)
Touch your thumb with your middle finger and repeat the push hand/push cow routine. Serve the steak when they feel the same.

Well-done (C)
Touch your thumb with your ring finger ... you know the drill.

NOTES / MODS

4

The only things stopping you from buying a brand spanking new, fancy cafe-style sandwich press is spare cash and bench space. If you're pressed for either, press your sandwich like this.

YOU WILL NEED:

(A) 1 can
(B) 1 plate
(C) 1 sandwich
(D) 1 frying pan

DIAGRAM 1

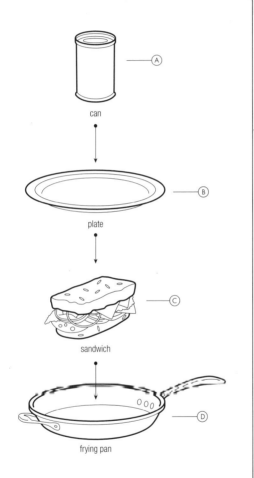

can

plate

sandwich

frying pan

PAN PRESS

HOW IT'S DONE:

Make a sandwich and spread some marg. on the outside of the bread.

Place the sandwich in the frying pan and throw it on the stove. Whack a plate on top of the sanga and weigh it down with a can.

Set the stove to low and fry the sandwich so the bottom toasts and the contents begin to warm. Keep an eye on the prize. Too much heat will burn the bottom.

Flip and repeat for the second side.

If you've made a monster, heat it through in the microwave before pressing it.

SEND YOUR QWIK FIXES TO
www.BeatHeatEat.com

FIRE FIGHTER

Fire. Food. Two things central to Man's survival. But things can turn nasty when there's too much of one and not enough of the other. If the kitchen is about to be redecorated Ash Wednesday style, it's way too late to be reading this. Run, Forrest, run!

YOU WILL NEED:
(A) to be cooking with a frying pan
(B) 1 pan lid or a larger frying pan
(C) a fat fire

HOW IT'S DONE:
If a fat fire erupts in a frying pan on the stove top (it's okay to briefly be awed by your handiwork), quickly cover the pan with a lid or a larger frying pan. This will smother the flames.

Never, ever use water on a fat fire.

DIAGRAM 1

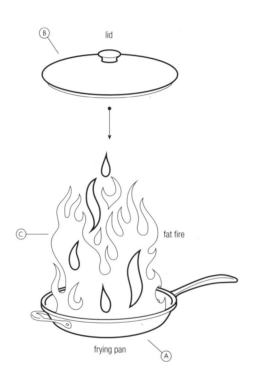

B   lid

C   fat fire

frying pan   A

NOTES / MODS

At some point this is going to happen. You can't avoid it. Accept the fact that you've applied enough heat to your dinner to make a sacrifice to the kitchen gods and move on.

YOU WILL NEED:

(A) dishwashing detergent

(B) a burnt mess in the bottom of a pot/frying pan

DIAGRAM 1

dishwashing detergent

burnt pan

HOW IT'S DONE:

Squirt a few drops of dishwashing detergent over the sacrifice and add enough water to cover the bottom of the pot/pan.

Bring the soapy water to a boil and your burnt offering will lift from the bottom.

BURN & LEARN

MICRO CLEANING

World domination starts at home. Give your nuclear arsenal a spit and polish from time to time to keep it in a ready state.

DIAGRAM 1

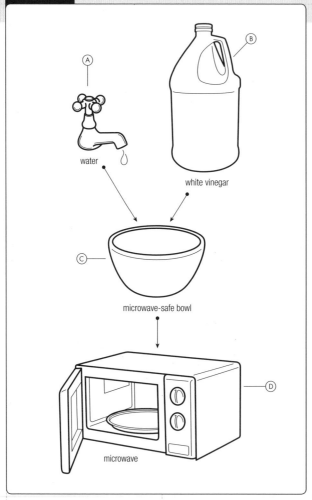

water

white vinegar

microwave-safe bowl

microwave

YOU WILL NEED:
(A) 1 cup water
(B) ½ cup white vinegar
(C) 1 microwave-safe bowl
(D) a messy microwave

HOW IT'S DONE:
Mix everything together in a large microwave-safe bowl.

Shove the bowl in the micro and heat that baby on high for a couple of minutes or so, or until the mixture boils. You want this to bubble away for about a minute – keep an eye on it so it doesn't boil over. Otherwise you're going to get an extra messy microwave to clean!

While the oven is still steamy, wipe down the insides with a cloth.

NOTES / MODS

Have you ever noticed a spoon has two ends? Have you ever noticed you only use the fat bit? Cut down on your spoon wastage and use the skinny end to stir with as well.

YOU WILL NEED:

(A) 1 spoon
(B) a couple of things to stir

DIAGRAM 1

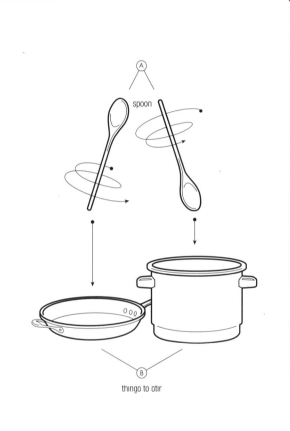

spoon

thingo to otir

HOW IT'S DONE:

OK. Say you've got a main meal on the burner and you're doing a little side dish as well.

Use the fat end of the spoon to do the heavy work on the mains.

When you need to whiz the side dish a bit, flip the spoon on its end and go your hardest.

2 SPOONS IN 1

SEND YOUR QWIK FIXES TO
www.BeatHeatEat.com

10

[SNAKS]

11

A bag of chips will disappear faster than an aspirin at a rave party. When your fingers come out of the bag covered only in the seasoning, it's time for Plan B.

DIAGRAM 1

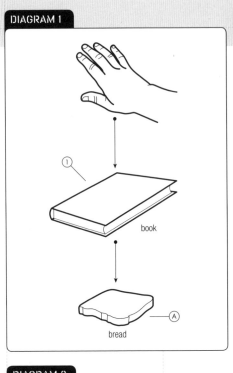

book

bread

Ⓐ

DIAGRAM 2

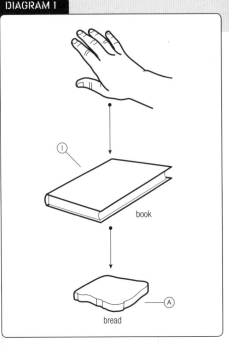

spray-on oil

②

DIAGRAM 3

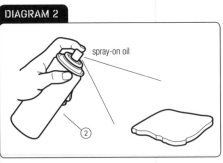

Ⓑ

french onion soup mix

③

DIAGRAM 4

baking tray

④

NOTES / MODS

SERVES: Heaps

PREP TIME: 5 minutes

COOK TIME: 5–10 minutes

PARTS:

(A) bread (sliced)
(B) 1 packet French onion soup mix

TOOLS:

(1) something flat (like this book)
(2) spray-on oil
(3) 1 large plate
(4) 1 baking tray

ASSEMBLY:

Squash the bread so it's thin – really thin. Whack a slice on the bench and grab the something flat (this book) and use it to squash the whiteness out of the bread.

Once you've got the bread looking like it's a finalist on *The Biggest Loser* give one side a good spray with the spray-on oil.

Sprinkle the French onion soup mix onto the large plate.

Push the oiled side of the bread slices into the soup mix. Check you've got a good covering and then place them on the baking tray.

Set the oven at about 180°C and bake these guys for 5–10 minutes. Keep an eye on them so they don't burn.

When the bread starts to darken they're good to go. Slice them up or go them whole.

TIP / OPTION

Have plenty of drinks on hand – these kids are SALTY.

If you're going to make these for Her, slice up a French stick into 3–5 mm pieces.

french stick

Just like the Ark, the ingredients in this recipe go in 2 by 2.

NOAH'S MUFFINS

DIAGRAM 1

PARTS:

(A) 2 cups self-raising flour

(B) 2 cups grated cheese

(C) 2 eggs

(D) 2 cups milk

MAKES: 8–12 muffins

PREP TIME: 15 minutes

COOK TIME: 20 minutes

TOOLS:

(1) a grater

(2) a bowl

(3) another bowl

(4) something greasy (spray-on oil, olive oil, margarine, etc)

(5) 1 muffin tray

You can tart these up by adding a few chilli flakes or some fresh herbs.

TIP / OPTION

ASSEMBLY:

Preheat oven to 200°C.

Mix the flour and cheese in a bowl.

Beat the eggs with the milk and add to the dry stuff until it's all sloshy and there's no dry flour left.

Spoon the mixture into muffin tray (first give the tray a good spray with some spray-on oil).

Bake for 20 minutes or until the muffins look golden on top.

If you want to quickly fry up some eggs but can't be bothered hauling everything out of the cupboard, give this a go. Clean up is easy too. Wipe over the sandwich toaster and bin the shells.

TOASTED EGGS

DIAGRAM 1

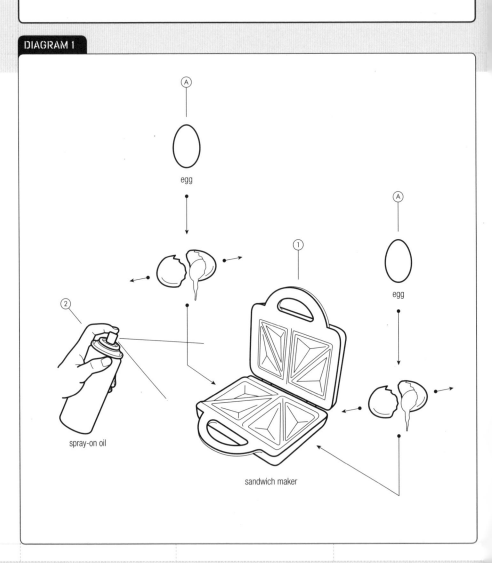

A

egg

2
spray-on oil

1

A

egg

sandwich maker

PARTS:

(A) 2 eggs

TOOLS:

(1) 1 sandwich maker
(2) something greasy (spray-on oil, olive oil, margarine, etc)

SERVES: 1

PREP TIME: 2 minutes – this includes getting the eggs from the fridge

COOK TIME: Ask your sandwich maker

ASSEMBLY:

Fire up the sandwich maker and give it a good spray with some spray-on oil.

Give it a few minutes and then crack an egg into each side.

If you want a runny yolk leave the lid open; for well-done kids, have the lid down.

When they're done, whack them on a plate and inhale.

Add bacon to one side for a bacon and egg brekky.

TIP / OPTION

You are going to score points with Her/Her Mum when you can rustle up a quick bit of chew. Bonus points will be given if you can produce a chilled bottle of Chardy as well. Serve these dips with any dry bikkies e.g. Salada.

DIAGRAM 1

(A) philadelphia cream cheese

(B) tuna in springwater

(1)

DIAGRAM 2

(A) plain yoghurt

(B) tikka masala curry paste

(1)

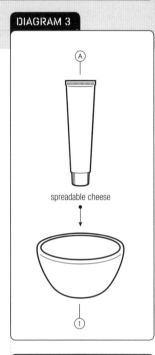

DIAGRAM 3

(A) spreadable cheese

(1)

DIAGRAM 1: TUNA DIP

PARTS:

(A) 1 150 g tub Philadelphia cream cheese

(B) 1 80 g can tuna in springwater

TOOLS:
(1) 1 bowl

ASSEMBLY:
Put the ingredients in a bowl. Mix. Eat.

For some extra zing, use chilli tuna instead or add some sweet chilli sauce.

NOTES / MODS

18

DIAGRAM 2: CURRY DIP

PARTS:

(A) 300 ml plain yoghurt

(B) 1/2 teaspoon Tikka Masala curry paste

TOOLS:

(1) 1 microwave-safe bowl

ASSEMBLY:

Put the paste in a small microwave-safe bowl and heat on low for 15 seconds. It's going to spit everywhere so put a cover on the bowl.

Dump in the yoghurt. Mix. Serve.

Use less yoghurt if you want extra zing.

SERVES: Enough to go around

PREP TIME: 1–2 minutes

COOK TIME: 15 seconds for the Curry Dip. Otherwise just mix and go

This keeps well in the fridge for a couple of days and, if anything, the flavour gets better.

TIP / OPTION

DIAGRAM 3: CHEESY DIP CHEAT

PARTS:

(A) Spreadable cheese (eg Kraft)

TOOLS:

(1) 1 small bowl

ASSEMBLY:

Empty the cheese into the bowl.

If anybody asks, don't tell.

TIP / OPTION

Sure – you can reach into a box of cereal for a quick handy snak. But go the extra yard and pimp your snak.

DIAGRAM 1

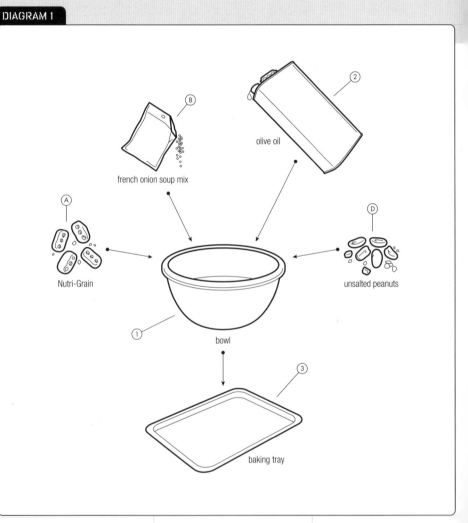

B
french onion soup mix

olive oil

2

A
Nutri-Grain

1
bowl

D
unsalted peanuts

3
baking tray

NOTES / MODS

PARTS:

(A) 3 cups Nutri-Grain cereal

(B) 2 cups unsalted peanuts

(C) 1 packet French onion soup mix

TOOLS:

(1) a bowl

(2) 100 ml olive oil

(3) 1 baking tray

SERVES: Enough to get you through the munchies

PREP TIME: 3–5 minutes

COOK TIME: 5–10 minutes

TIP / OPTION

Store any leftovers in an airtight container.

ASSEMBLY:

Get the oven going at about 180°C.

Throw all the ingredients in a bowl and give them a good mix.

When everything looks nice and messed up, tip everything onto one of those flat baking trays and hurl it in the oven.

Give everything a bit of a turn over every couple of minutes or so.

It will be ready in 5–10 minutes. Watch for when the Nutri-Grain starts to darken and you're just about ready.

Go them when they've cooled down.

T he next time you have friends around for a BBQ, throw extra snags on the hot plate. Even with a hangover these sausage rolls are really easy to put together the next day.

DIAGRAM 1

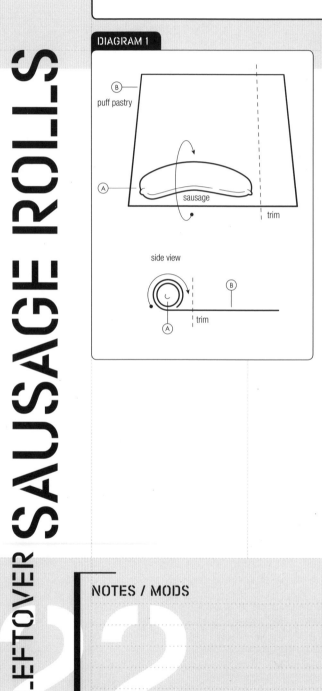

B — puff pastry

A — sausage

trim

side view

B

trim

A

DIAGRAM 2

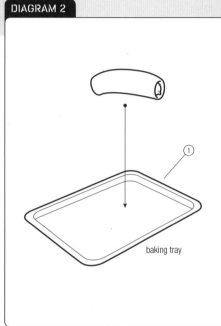

baking tray

[**NOTES / MODS**

PARTS:

(A) a bunch of leftover sausages

(B) puff pastry

TOOLS:

(1) 1 baking tray

SERVES: To keep everyone happy, allow 2 snags per person

PREP TIME: 30 seconds per roll

COOK TIME: 15–20 minutes

ASSEMBLY:

Remove the plastic sheet from in-between the pastry.

Line up your snag with the edge of the pastry and trim any excess width off the pastry.

Roll the sausage over (hence the name) so it's wrapped in pastry. Trim again, allowing for a little overlap.

Repeat this until you're out of sausages, or out of pastry.

Whack these on the baking tray and into the oven for 15–20 minutes or so on 200°C. Bake them until your mouth starts watering and the pastry starts looking golden brown.

TIP / OPTION

Serve with sauce.
You'll have a lot of pastry off-cuts as you work through your sausages. Keep them and wrap your remaining snags like an Egyptian mummy.

SAVE MANKIND. POST YOUR MODS AND RECIPES AT **www.BeatHeatEat.com**

[MAINS]

25

You're not going to find this dish in any self-respecting kitchen – that's why you are going to make it in yours. Give in to the Dark Side.

COKE CHICKEN

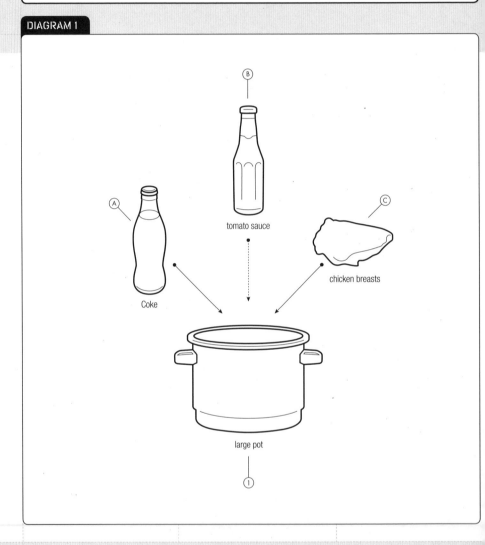

DIAGRAM 1

Ⓐ Coke

Ⓑ tomato sauce

Ⓒ chicken breasts

① large pot

NOTES / MODS

PARTS:

(A) 1 litre Coke

(B) tomato sauce (optional)

(C) 4 chicken breasts
      (or similar quantity of drumsticks and/or wings)

TOOLS:

(1) 1 large pot

ASSEMBLY:

Mix together the Coke and tomato sauce in a
large pot. Use 2 glugs of sauce for each chicken
breast or 1 glug for each wing or drumstick.
And 1 for good luck.

Heat this on the stove top on high until it bubbles,
then turn it down to low.

Throw in the chook and poke it about to cover
it in the liquid.

Simmer uncovered for 45 minutes to 1 hour.

Don't worry about this being soupy at first.
The Coke thickens as it cooks.

SERVES: 4

PREP TIME: 5 minutes

COOK TIME: Somewhere between
45 minutes and 1 hour

TIP / OPTION

*Pork chops can be cooked in the
same way.*

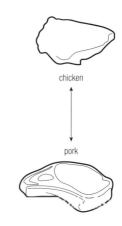

chicken

↑
↓

pork

CRUNCHY CHICKEN

You can do a lot with chicken. But then again, why would you?

DIAGRAM 1

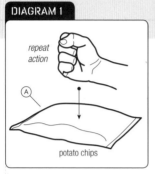

repeat action

A

potato chips

DIAGRAM 2

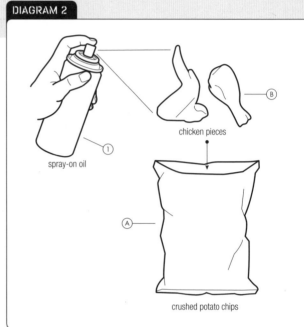

spray-on oil (1)

chicken pieces (B)

A

crushed potato chips

DIAGRAM 3

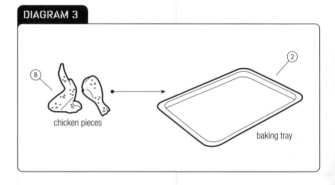

B chicken pieces

(2) baking tray

NOTES / MODS

PARTS:
(A) 1 bag potato chips
(B) chicken pieces – as many as you want

TOOLS:
(1) spray-on oil
(2) 1 baking tray

SERVES: Buy enough chicken and chips and you can feed everyone

PREP TIME: Not long

COOK TIME: 20 minutes or so

ASSEMBLY:
Before opening the bag of chips, give them a good crushing.

Lightly squirt the chicken pieces all over with just enough spray-on oil to make them sticky. Drop them into the bag of chips.

Give the bag a good shaking. Pull the bird bits out and place them on the baking tray.

Aim the tray at the oven and bake the chicken for 20 minutes on 200°C. Make sure the chicken is cooked through before eating. Life's too short for eating pink chicken. Remember the Golden Rule of chicken cooking – 'if it's all white, it's all right'.

TIP / OPTION

No spray? No problem. Drop a little oil on the chicken pieces and coat them by hand.

Use sweet chilli sauce as a spicy alternative.

If you line the tray with alfoil, you don't need to clean it. Throw the alfoil in the recycling bin and the tray in the cupboard.

Leave the athletes to suck down the oranges at half time. You, my friend, are going to suck down a flaky, golden-brown parcel of meaty delight. Cook it through the long break and you'll be good to go for the second half.

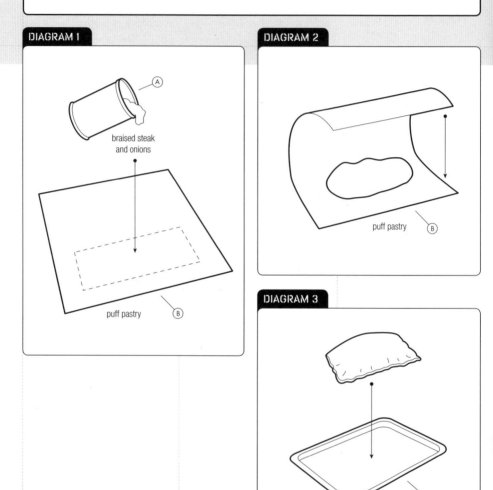

DIAGRAM 1

braised steak and onions

puff pastry

DIAGRAM 2

puff pastry

DIAGRAM 3

baking tray

NOTES / MODS

PARTS:
(A) 1 410 g can braised steak and onions
(B) 1 sheet puff pastry

TOOLS:
(1) 1 baking tray

ASSEMBLY:

In the ad break before half time, pull the puff pastry out of the freezer to defrost.

When the siren goes, tear the top off the braised steak and onions and aim the contents towards one edge of the pastry.

Fold the pastry over, jamming the edges together.

Throw it on the baking tray and into the oven for 20 minutes on 200°C. Pull it out and watch the second half.

Serve with sauce.

SERVES: Makes 1 BIG pie

PREP TIME: A couple of minutes, plus thawing

COOK TIME: 20 minutes

You can also use a can of chunky-style soup. Drain off as much liquid as you can before dumping it on the pastry.

TIP / OPTION

FAST FISH

This is the ultimate fast food. There's hardly any prep and next to zero clean up. This is a great dish to make for Her.

DIAGRAM 1

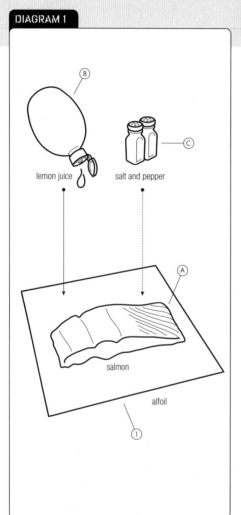

lemon juice

salt and pepper

salmon

alfoil

DIAGRAM 2

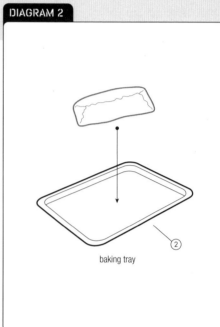

baking tray

NOTES / MODS

PARTS:

(A) a nice meaty piece of fish
   (salmon, flake, tuna, etc)
(B) lemon juice
(C) salt and pepper (optional)

TOOLS:

(1) alfoil
(2) 1 baking tray

ASSEMBLY:

Place the fish in the middle of the alfoil.

Squirt some lemon juice over it and add a little seasoning.

Bring the edges of the alfoil together in the middle so the fish is wrapped up.

Put the fish on the baking tray and into the oven for 10–15 minutes at 180°C.

SERVES: 1 fillet will do for 1 person

PREP TIME: 1–2 minutes

COOK TIME: 10–15 minutes depending on the size of the piece of fish

Keep Her happy and serve this with some steamed vegies.

TIP / OPTION

SOUPER PASTA

Making pasta is as easy as boiling water. Making a sauce to go with it is as easy as opening a can of soup.

DIAGRAM 1

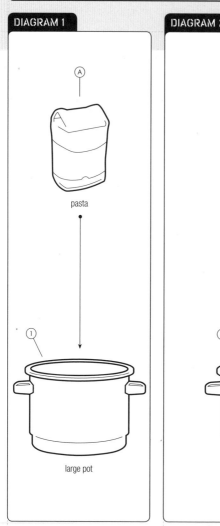

A

pasta

① large pot

DIAGRAM 2

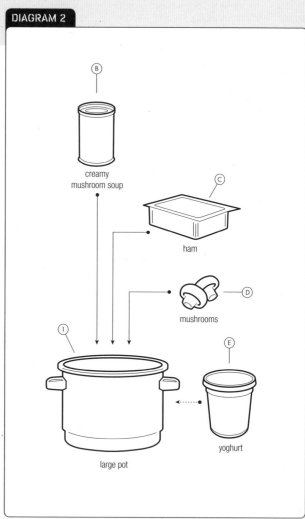

B

creamy mushroom soup

C ham

D mushrooms

E yoghurt

① large pot

NOTES / MODS

34

PARTS:

(A) your choice of pasta

(B) 1 420 g can creamy mushroom soup

(C) 1 100 g pack of ham

(D) 4–5 mushrooms

(E) yoghurt (optional)

(F) cheese (optional)

TOOLS:

(1) 1 large pot

(2) 2 bowls

(3) 1 grater

ASSEMBLY:

Cook 500 g pasta according to the directions on the packet.

While this is simmering away, start slicing up the ham and mushrooms.

When the pasta is cooked, strain it and dump it back into the pot. Hurl in the soup, ham and mushrooms and mix everything together over a LOW heat for a couple of minutes.

Once everything is warmed through, tip everything into a couple of bowls.

Serve with grated cheese.

SERVES: 2 if you're hungry.
More if you want to stretch it

PREP TIME: 5 minutes

COOK TIME: See the pasta pack + a couple of minutes to mix it all together

For a little extra something, stir a couple of dollops of plain yoghurt through at the end.

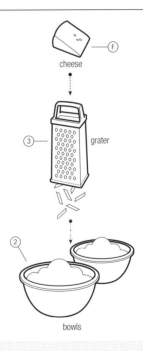

cheese

grater

bowls

STICKY CHICKEN

She doesn't have to know what a tight arse you are so, instead of taking Her out to dinner, impress Her and invite Her around to your place. Nothing fancy of course, but She'll be impressed you've made an effort. Have a brekky plan in place just in case.

DIAGRAM 1

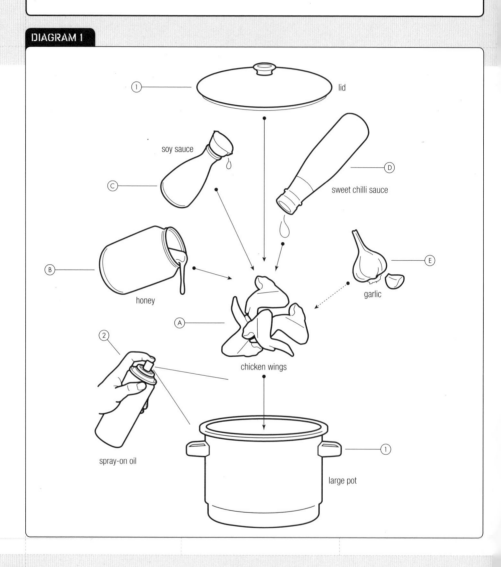

- 1 — lid
- soy sauce
- C
- D — sweet chilli sauce
- B
- honey
- E — garlic
- A — chicken wings
- 2 — spray-on oil
- 1 — large pot

NOTES / MODS

PARTS:

(A) 8 or so pieces of chicken
(drumsticks, wings or both)
(B) soy sauce
(C) honey
(D) sweet chilli sauce
(E) garlic, chopped (optional, but good to add)

SERVES: Her and yourself

PREP TIME: 8 minutes

COOK TIME: 30–40 minutes

TOOLS:

(1) 1 large pot (with a lid) or frying pan
(2) something greasy (spray-on oil, olive oil,
margarine, etc)

Tip / Option

This is a dish you can make for Her. It's best eaten with fingers, so show Her how considerate you are and give Her a napkin. It's also a good idea to have a spare bowl to put the bones in.

Serve the wings in a bowl. That way She can help Herself.

If you're really keen, you can prep this dish the day before, leaving it to marinate overnight in the fridge.

ASSEMBLY:

Grab the frying pan or pot, give it a quick grease up, and throw it on the stove. Set it to max.

Lob in the chicken.

Go the soy sauce and give each piece 2–3 squirts, then drizzle a line of honey down everything.

Run some sweet chilli sauce around the pot once or twice, and add the garlic if you've got it handy.

Turn the heat down LOW and place a lid on the pot/pan. Use a large plate if you don't have a lid nearby.

Slow cooking is the key here. Let everything simmer away for 30–40 minutes or until the wings are cooked. Don't rush. Go and watch TV.

Stir the pot/pan in ad breaks. With about 15 minutes to go, take the lid off so the liquid thickens. If it starts to do this early, add a bit more soy sauce.

Here's something you can burn. The key to this is ventilation, ventilation, ventilation. This is best made outdoors but if you're going to have a crack at it in the kitchen, open the window and take the batteries out of the smoke alarm (but remember to put them back in afterwards).

DIAGRAM 1

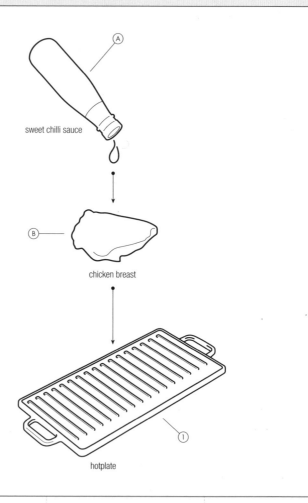

sweet chilli sauce

A

chicken breast

B

hotplate

1

NOTES / MODS

PARTS:

(A) sweet chilli sauce

(B) chicken breasts – as many as you can eat

TOOLS:

(1) 1 hotplate

ASSEMBLY:

Slap the breasts onto a hotplate and smother one side in sweet chilli sauce.

Cook for 8–10 minutes then flip and repeat for the second side.

When the sauce hits the hotplate it's going to smoke and burn. This is good a thing. Knock off any large burnt pieces of sauce as you go. If you have a ridged hotplate your chicken will have an authentic chargrilled appearance.

Make sure the chicken is cooked all the way through before eating it (it should look white). If it's got a pink tinge, leave it on the hotplate a bit longer.

SERVES: A breast will do 1 person

PREP TIME: As fast as you can slap a chicken breast on a hotplate

COOK TIME: About 20 minutes

TIP / OPTION

If the smoke is too much, smother the breast in sweet chilli sauce, wrap it in alfoil and bung in the oven for 20 minutes or so. It won't have the grilled look but it'll still taste okay.

If there's only one thing you make from this book make sure it's this one. I know people who do their Christmas turkey this way by stuffing enough bread inside the cavity to hold the can in place.

DIAGRAM 1

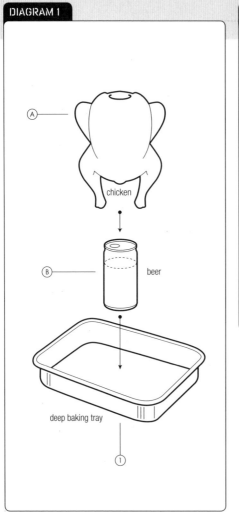

Ⓐ chicken

Ⓑ beer

deep baking tray

①

DIAGRAM 2

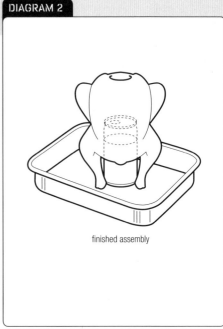

finished assembly

NOTES / MODS

PARTS:

(A) 1 whole chicken

(B) 1 can beer of your choice

TOOLS:

(1) 1 deep baking tray

SERVES: Enough for now and some for later

PREP TIME: 5 minutes

COOK TIME: 90 minutes

ASSEMBLY:

Rinse the chicken inside and out (cleaning as much gunk from the cavity as possible) and pat dry with some paper towel.

Crack the tinnie open and pour about $\frac{1}{3}$ out.

Insert the can into the bird's cavity and place everything on the baking tray.

Stand back and admire your work. Drink the glass of beer.

Carefully place the assembly into an oven and bake on 200°C for 90 minutes or until the chicken is cooked.

The can is going to be hot when the bird is cooked – be careful when you remove it.

You can make the skin go nice and crispy by spraying the bird with olive oil before it goes into the oven.

You might as well throw the seasoning of your choice at it while you're there.

TIP / OPTION

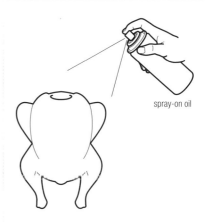

spray-on oil

These are fast and simple to make. Perfect for when you just want to beat, heat and eat.

DIAGRAM 1

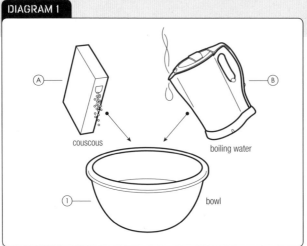

Ⓐ couscous
Ⓑ boiling water
① bowl

DIAGRAM 2

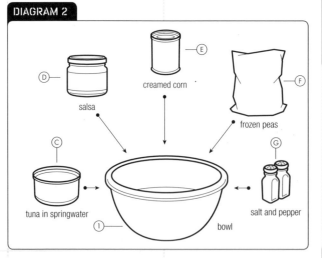

Ⓓ salsa
Ⓔ creamed corn
Ⓕ frozen peas
Ⓒ tuna in springwater
Ⓖ salt and pepper
① bowl

DIAGRAMS 3 - 6

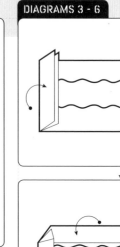

Ⓗ

seam side up

flip to bake

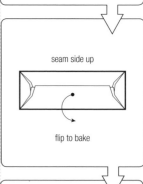

② baking tray

NOTES / MODS

42

PARTS:

(A) 4 or 5 handfuls couscous

(B) boiling water

(C) 1 425 g can tuna in springwater

(D) 375 g jar salsa

(E) 1 310 g can creamed corn

(F) 4 or 5 handfuls frozen peas

(G) salt and pepper to taste

(H) 1 packet mountain bread (or similar flat bread)

TOOLS:

(1) 1 bowl

(2) 1 baking tray

ASSEMBLY:

Throw the couscous into a bowl and pour in just enough boiling water to cover the top of it. Whack something like a plate on top of the bowl and wait for a couple of minutes for all the water to be absorbed.

Give the couscous a stir through to break it up. Dump the remaining parts, except the mountain bread, into the bowl and mix together.

To make the wraps you'll need a double layer of mountain bread to avoid the casing splitting. Grab two sheets of mountain bread and stack about a 1/4 of the mixture into the middle.

Bring the left and right sides of the mountain bread towards the middle. Now do the same with the top and bottom sides so the mixture is enclosed.

Flip the wrap upside down so the seam is on the bottom and place on a baking tray. This will help keep the seam shut. Bake these kids for 20 minutes on 200°C.

Serve with sauce.

SERVES: This recipe will make 4 wraps. 1 will do for 1 person unless you're hungry

PREP TIME: 10 minutes

COOK TIME: 20 minutes

TIP / OPTION

Drain the tuna by opening the can and pushing the lid in so the liquid is forced out.

If you haven't got an hour to spare waiting for the dough to rise, see the next page. Otherwise, read on – it's worth the wait.

DIAGRAM 1

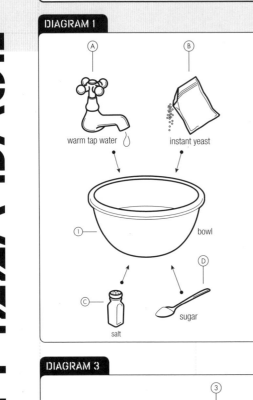

Ⓐ warm tap water

Ⓑ instant yeast

① bowl

Ⓒ salt

Ⓓ sugar

DIAGRAM 2

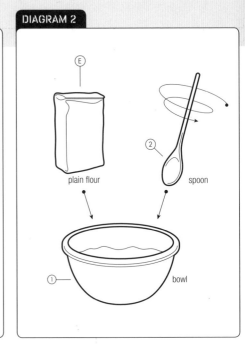

Ⓔ plain flour

② spoon

① bowl

DIAGRAM 3

③ cling wrap

DIAGRAM 4

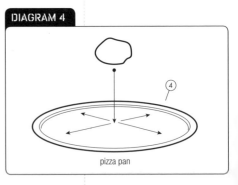

④ pizza pan

NOTES / MODS

PARTS: *Will make 1 thick or 2 thin bases*

(A) 1 cup warm tap water
(B) 2 sachets instant yeast
(C) a little bit of salt
(D) a similar amount of sugar
(E) 2 cups plain flour

SERVES: Easy big fella. 1 pizza per person will do it

PREP TIME: Including the wait ... 75 minutes + making the pizza

COOK TIME: 20–30 minutes

TOOLS:

(1) 1 bowl
(2) a spoon
(3) cling wrap
(4) 1 pizza pan (or baking tray)

ASSEMBLY:

Mix together the water, yeast, salt and sugar in a bowl. Let this sit for 10 minutes so it goes frothy.

Dump in the flour and mix together to form a ball. You are looking for something that resembles a dough-like substance. If the mix is too dry, add a dash of water; too wet, add a bit of flour.

Right, now let this kid rise for 60 minutes. You can aid the process by throwing some Glad Wrap over the bowl.

When it's ready, sprinkle some extra flour on your work bench and tip the dough out, rolling it around in the flour. This will allow you to pick it up without it sticking to your hands. If it's still sticky, add a bit more flour and keep rolling.

Oil up your pizza pan or baking tray and flatten the base until it reaches the edge, sprinkling on a little flour whenever it starts to get sticky.

Add your toppings and bake for 20–30 minutes or until done.

Keep an eye on things and turn the pizza around midway through cooking.

TIP / OPTION

Turn the oven on to 200°C when you start rolling out the base. You want it to be REALLY hot when the pizza goes in.

Grab a tub with a lid and throw in the toppings as you cut them up. Whack the lid on and give it a good shake. This will mix everything up nicely and give your pizza an easy 'just got out of bed' look. Place any meat and cheese on separately though as they can clump together in the tub.

repeat action

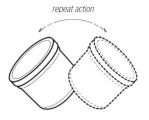

EZ-ER PIZZA BASE

We're only giving you the base here – the toppings are up to you. Pile it high or go lean and mean. What a man does with his pizza toppings in the privacy of his home is his own business.

DIAGRAM 1

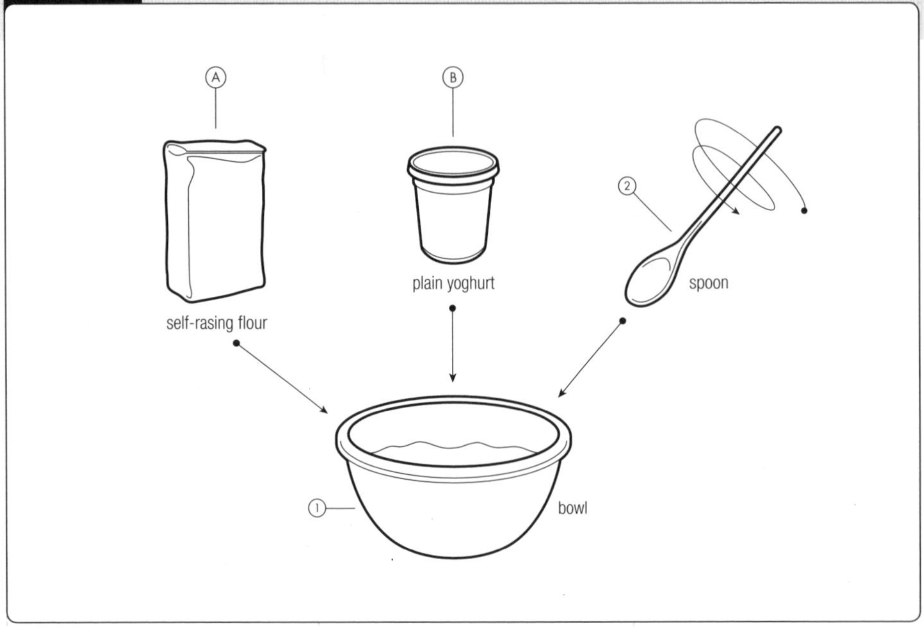

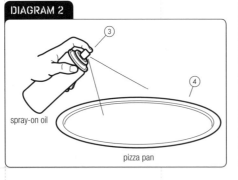

A
B
self-rasing flour
plain yoghurt
2
spoon
1
bowl

DIAGRAM 2

3
4
spray-on oil
pizza pan

DIAGRAM 3

4
pizza pan

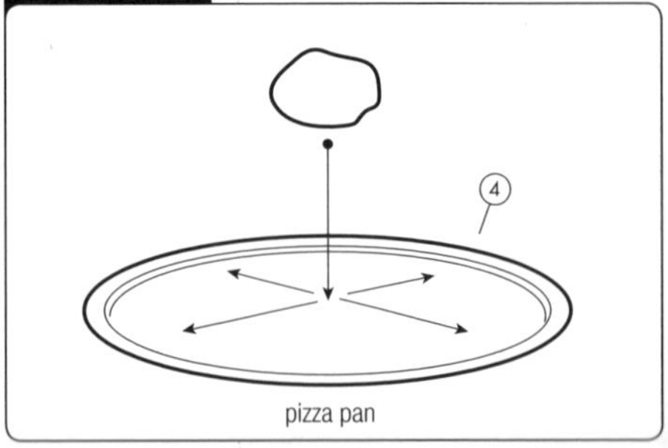

NOTES / MODS

PARTS:

(A) 1 ½ cups self-raising flour

(B) 200 ml plain yoghurt

SERVES: 1 base, 1 person

PREP TIME: 10 minutes for the base. Longer to add the toppings

COOK TIME: 20–30 minutes for the whole shebang. See previous spread

TOOLS:

(1) 1 bowl

(2) a spoon

(3) something greasy (spray-on oil, olive oil, margarine, etc)

(4) 1 pizza pan (or baking tray)

If the mixture is too wet add a little more flour; too dry, add a little more yoghurt.

TIP / OPTION

ASSEMBLY:

Dump everything into a bowl and mix together.

Once the mix gets to a doughy consistency, roll it out onto the greased pizza pan or baking tray and flatten the base until it reaches the edge, sprinkling on a little flour whenever it starts to get sticky.

Now add your toppings and get this baby in the oven for 20–30 minutes.

SOUPER PORK

This is a great dish to make after a long day. You can throw everything together really easily and then kick back.

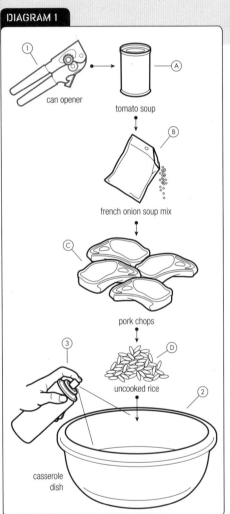

DIAGRAM 1

① can opener → tomato soup (A)

french onion soup mix (B)

pork chops (C)

uncooked rice (D)

③

casserole dish (2)

DIAGRAM 2

water (E)

empty tomato soup can (A)

casserole dish (2)

NOTES / MODS

PARTS:

(A) 1 420 g can tomato soup

(B) 1 packet French onion soup mix

(C) 2 large or 4 small pork chops

(D) ½ cup (or so) uncooked rice

(E) 1 can water

SERVES: 2. Really

PREP TIME: 5 minutes

COOK TIME: 90 minutes

TOOLS:

(1) 1 can opener

(2) 1 casserole dish (with lid)

(3) something greasy (spray-on oil, olive oil, margarine, etc)

ASSEMBLY:

Grease a casserole dish with something greasy. Throw in the rice.

Place the pork chops on top of the rice.

Sprinkle the French onion soup mix over the chops.

Dump the can of tomato soup over the lot.

Add 1 can of water (use the empty soup can).

Give everything a bit of a stir.

Cover and bake for 90 minutes at 180°C. Give everything another stir midway through cooking.

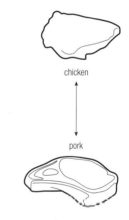

chicken

↕

pork

Don't be fooled by the number of parts in this dish. Most of them are easily found on your supermarket shelf.

CHILLI BEANS

DIAGRAM 1

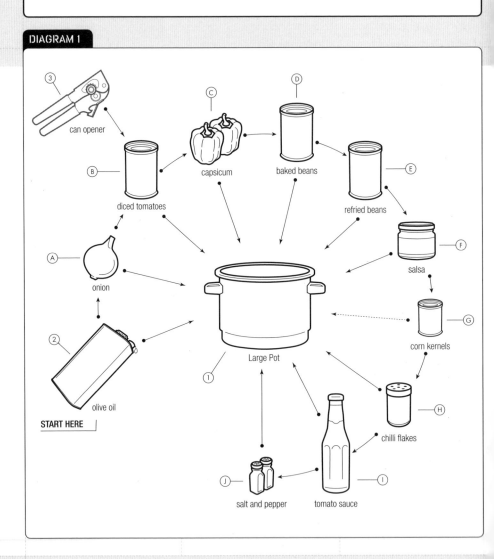

③ can opener

Ⓒ capsicum

Ⓓ baked beans

Ⓑ diced tomatoes

Ⓔ

refried beans

Ⓐ onion

Ⓕ salsa

② olive oil

Ⓖ corn kernels

START HERE

Large Pot

Ⓘ

Ⓗ chilli flakes

Ⓙ salt and pepper

Ⓘ tomato sauce

NOTES / MODS

PARTS:

(A) 1 medium onion
(B) 1 400 g can diced tomatoes
(C) 2 capsicums (1 red, 1 green)
(D) 1 420 g can baked beans
(E) 1 435 g can refried beans
(F) 1 375 g jar salsa
(G) 1 310 g can corn kernels (optional)
(H) chilli flakes to taste
(I) tomato sauce
(J) salt and pepper to taste
(K) cheese (optional)

TOOLS:

(1) 1 large pot (with lid)
(2) something greasy
   (spray-on oil, olive oil,
   margarine, etc)
(3) 1 can opener
(4) 1 grater
(5) 1 bowl

ASSEMBLY:

Chop the onion and throw it in the pot with a little olive oil. Cook this on a high heat.

When the onions are starting to brown, open the diced tomatoes and add them to the onion. Turn the heat to low.

Start chopping the capsicums and opening the cans.

After the onions and tomatoes have been cooking for a couple of minutes, add the rest of the parts, with 4 or 5 good glugs of tomato sauce, and mix together.

Whack a lid over the pot and simmer for 20 minutes or so, stirring occasionally.

When it's done, dump it into a bowl and grate some cheese over the top.

SERVES: Enough for 3 days

PREP TIME: 10 minutes

COOK TIME: 20 minutes

This dish will keep in the fridge for up to 3 days with the flavour improving over time. A great dish to make once and eat often.

TIP / OPTION

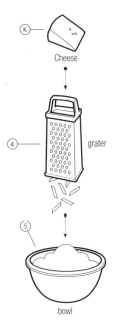

K — Cheese
4 — grater
5 — bowl

3-2-1 RIBS

A classic dish for the modern caveman to make.

DIAGRAM 1

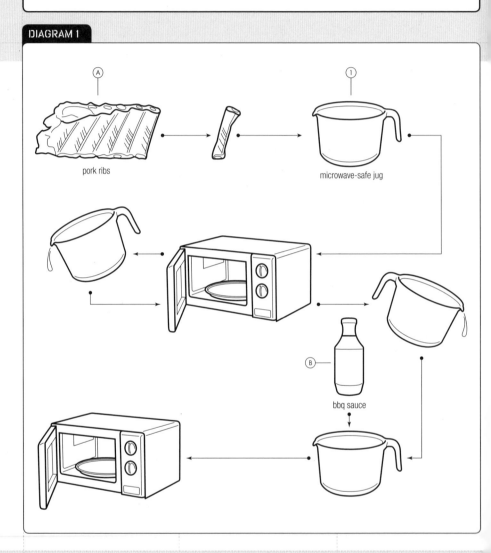

pork ribs

microwave-safe jug

bbq sauce

NOTES / MODS

52

PARTS:

(A) 1 rack pork ribs

(B) BBQ sauce

TOOLS:

(1) 1 microwave-safe jug, or bowl

SERVES: 1. There isn't much on a rib

PREP TIME: Next to nothing

COOK TIME: 6 minutes in the microwave

ASSEMBLY:

Cut the rack into individual ribs and place into a microwave-safe jug.

Nuke them on high for 3 minutes. Drain the fat from the jug.

Nuke again for 2 minutes. Drain any remaining fat.

Dump a generous amount of BBQ sauce over the ribs. Poke them around with a fork to make sure they're all coated.

Nuke again for 1 minute.

Eat.

These guys are REAL messy. Have something handy to wipe your hands and mouth with.

TIP / OPTION

BOY BURGERS

The problem with burger-joint burgers is they're never big enough to match your appetite. Make your own mammoth-sized monster and see if Man can conquer beast.

DIAGRAM 1

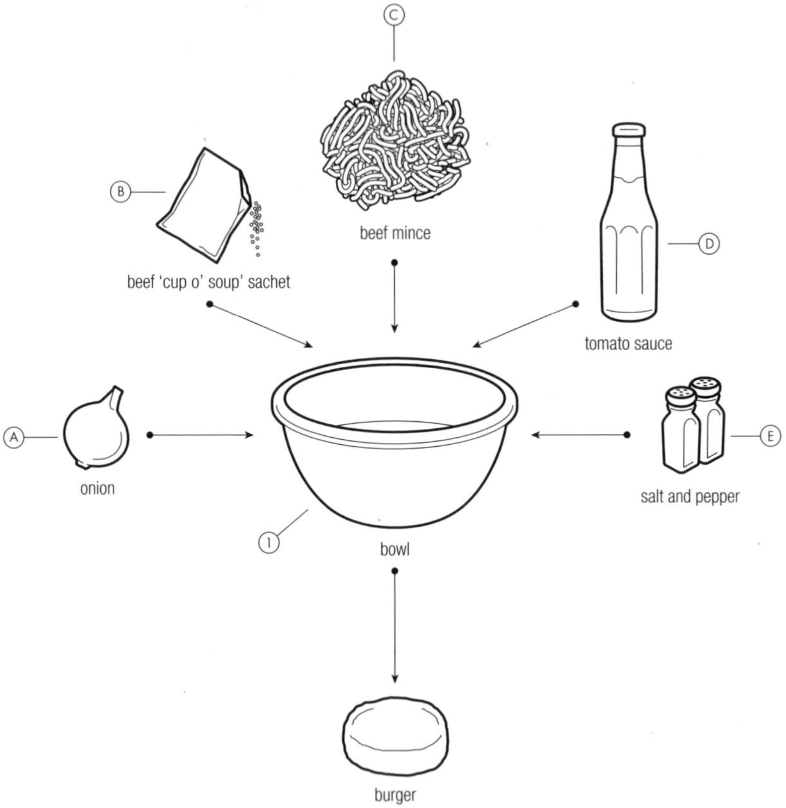

C

B

beef 'cup o' soup' sachet

beef mince

D

tomato sauce

A

onion

1

bowl

E

salt and pepper

burger

NOTES / MODS

54

PARTS:

(A) 1 onion

(B) 2 sachets beef-flavoured Cup o' Soup

(C) 400 g beef mince

(D) tomato sauce

(E) salt and pepper to taste

SERVES: 4. Less if you're up for a challenge

PREP TIME: 5–10 minutes

COOK TIME: Long enough for the burger to cook through

TOOLS:

(1) 1 bowl

ASSEMBLY:

Chop the onion into small bits. Throw the chopped onion and everything else into a bowl with 3–4 glugs of tomato sauce, and give it a good mix.

Form into as many burgers as you like and apply heat. Baking, frying or BBQ-ing will work best. Turn off the heat when they're cooked through.

Bun up and tackle.

Heads up – these guys will be a little crumbly. Cracking an egg and mixing it through with everything else will help.

You can also beef these up by adding grated carrot or zucchini to the mix.

TIP / OPTION

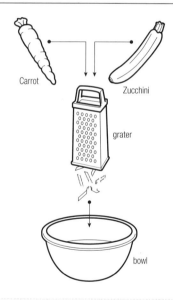

Carrot

Zucchini

grater

bowl

MEATBALLS

Easy to make and hard to mess up, this dish is a great thing to make on a Sunday night.

DIAGRAM 1

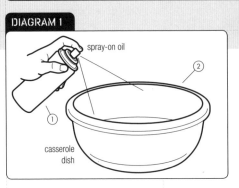

spray-on oil

② casserole dish

①

DIAGRAM 2

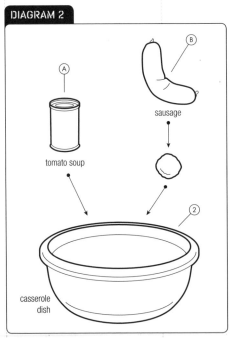

Ⓐ tomato soup

Ⓑ sausage

②

casserole dish

DIAGRAM 3

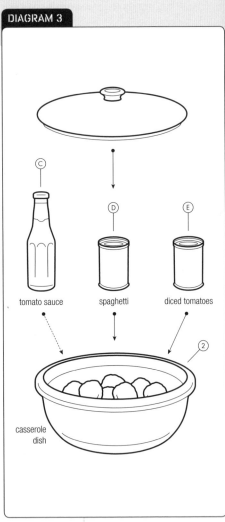

Ⓒ tomato sauce

Ⓓ spaghetti

Ⓔ diced tomatoes

②

casserole dish

NOTES / MODS

PARTS:

(A) 1 400 g can tomato soup

(B) sausages (flavour of your choice)

(C) tomato sauce (optional)

(D) 1 420 g can spaghetti

(E) 1 400 g can diced tomatoes (optional)

TOOLS:

(1) something greasy (spray-on oil, olive oil, margarine, etc)

(2) 1 casserole dish (with a lid)

ASSEMBLY:

Whack the oven on at 180°C and grease up the casserole dish.

Tear the lid off the soup and dump it into the bowl.

Now squeeze the meat out of the sausages and form into balls. You'll get 2 balls per snag. Drop them into the dish.

If you're going to add the sauce, drop a dob on each meatball now.

Dump the spaghetti over the top, followed by the diced tomatoes. Give everything a bit of a mix.

Put the lid on the casserole dish and poke it into the oven for 90 minutes. Give everything a prod about halfway through cooking.

SERVES: 2 – but don't pull this one out on your first date

PREP TIME: 10–15 minutes

COOK TIME: 90 minutes

TIP / OPTION

Grate a bit of cheese over the top.

Add a 420 g can of diced or crushed tomatoes to make the dish extra tomatoey.

Place a tray on the rack below the dish. If everything bubbles over, the tray will catch it, saving you the drama of cleaning the oven.

PEANUT CHICKEN

58

You can't beat an authentic Indian curry – that's why we choose not to compete. This is a dish any peanut can make.

DIAGRAM 1

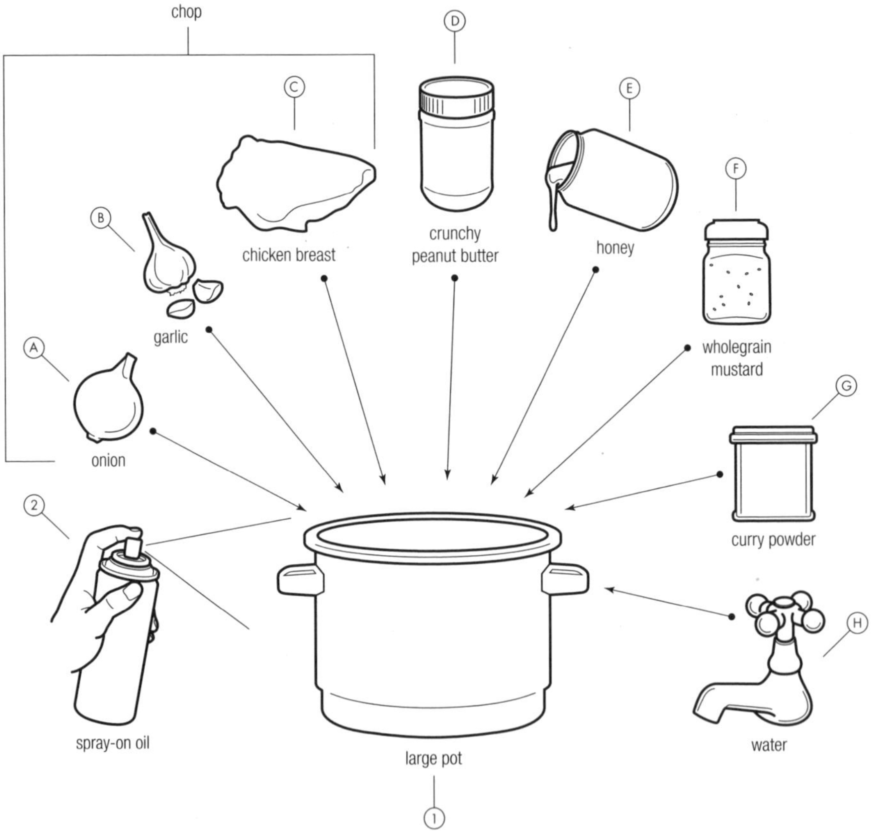
chop
C
chicken breast
D
crunchy
peanut butter
E
honey
F
wholegrain
mustard
B
garlic
A
onion
G
curry powder
2
spray-on oil
large pot
1
H
water

NOTES / MODS

PARTS:

(A) 1 onion

(B) 3 cloves of garlic (optional)

(C) 2 chicken breasts

(D) $\frac{1}{2}$ cup crunchy peanut butter

(E) $\frac{1}{2}$ cup honey

(F) 4 teaspoons wholegrain mustard

(G) 2 teaspoons curry powder

(H) 1 cup water

SERVES: 4 or 2 really hungry guys

PREP TIME: 5–10 minutes

COOK TIME: 15 minutes or so

TOOLS:

(1) 1 large pot (or frying pan)

(2) something greasy (spray-on oil, olive oil, margarine, etc)

This dish is best mates with rice.

See the rice packet. It will tell you what to do.

TIP / OPTION

ASSEMBLY:

Chop the chicken into bite-size pieces, then do the same with the onion and garlic but make them tiny, tiny pieces.

Oil up the pot or frying pan and cook the onion and garlic over a medium heat.

When the onion begins to look soft, add everything else.

Stir over a medium heat for 15 minutes or so, or until the chicken is done.

GIRL BURGERS

A cleverly disguised version of the Boy Burger styled especially for Her. If you really want to impress, serve this with minted yoghurt. If it's your first time, don't bang on about how you managed to hunt down the mint all by yourself. No matter how engaging you make the story, she won't be impressed.

DIAGRAM 1

A salmon
B instant oats
C egg
D curry powder
burger

DIAGRAM 2

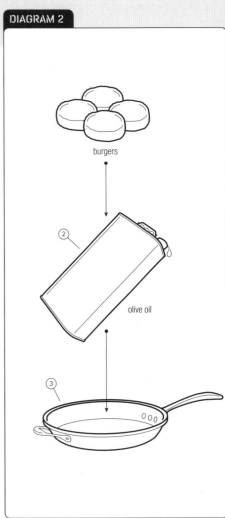

burgers
olive oil

NOTES / MODS

PARTS:

(A) 1 210 g can salmon, drained and flaked

(B) ⅓ cup instant oats

(C) 1 egg

(D) 2 – 3 teaspoons curry powder

TOOLS:

(1) 1 bowl

(2) something greasy (spray-on oil, olive oil, margarine, etc)

(3) 1 frying pan

ASSEMBLY:

Grab a bowl and dump everything into it, giving it a good mix.

Divide the mixture into 4 and flatten each portion into a flat patty shape.

Heat a little oil in a frying pan and cook each side of the patties for 3 minutes, or until browned and cooked through.

If your pan is sitting in the sink, you can throw these guys in the oven for 20 minutes on 180°C.

SERVES: I'm guessing you and Her

PREP TIME: 5 minutes

COOK TIME: Pan – a few minutes
Oven – 20 minutes on 180°C

TIP / OPTION

Minted yoghurt: Mix together 200 g plain yoghurt with ⅓ cup finely chopped mint.

Drain the salmon by opening the can and pushing the lid in so the liquid is forced out.

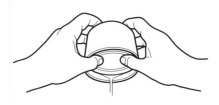

If your butcher doesn't already sell beef strips, get him to slice some up for you. The last thing you want on your conscience is the desecration of a perfect steak.

BEEF & BROC

DIAGRAM 1

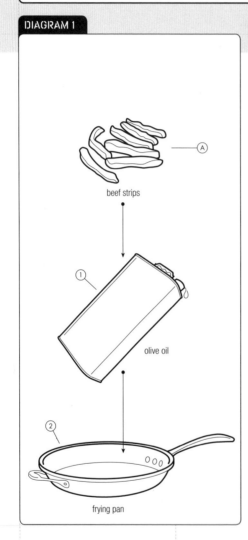

A — beef strips

1 olive oil

2 frying pan

DIAGRAM 2

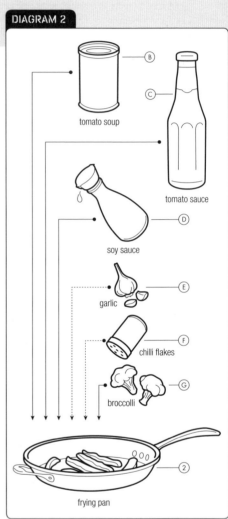

B — tomato soup

C — tomato sauce

D — soy sauce

E — garlic

F — chilli flakes

G — broccolli

2 frying pan

PARTS:

(A) 300 g beef strips
(B) 1 420 g can condensed tomato soup
(C) tomato sauce
(D) soy sauce
(E) a clove or two of garlic, chopped (optional)
(F) chilli flakes to taste (optional)
(G) sliced broccoli

SERVES: Makes 2 meals

PREP TIME: Really quick. Quicker if you've already got your beef sliced

COOK TIME: 10–15 minutes

TOOLS:

(1) something greasy (spray-on oil, olive oil, margarine, etc)
(2) 1 frying pan

TIP / OPTION

Don't mess about trying to peel the papery skin off the garlic.

Place a clove under a large flat knife and whack it. The skin can easily be removed and the garlic is nicely crushed for you to chop.

Be careful not to cut yourself.

ASSEMBLY:

Throw a frying pan down over medium heat and cook the beef strips in a little oil until they're browned.

Dump in the soup, 2–3 good glugs of tomato sauce, a healthy dose of soy sauce, garlic and chilli flakes. Turn up the heat until everything starts to bubble.

Add the broccoli and back off to a medium heat.

Keep stirring everything until the broccoli is kind of tender, but still crisp.

Serve over rice.

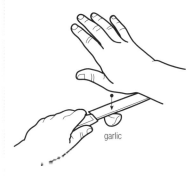

garlic

CHOP 'N' GO

D o your Mum proud and have a crack at a roast. She'll be rapt you're not only eating vegies but cooking them as well.

DIAGRAM 1

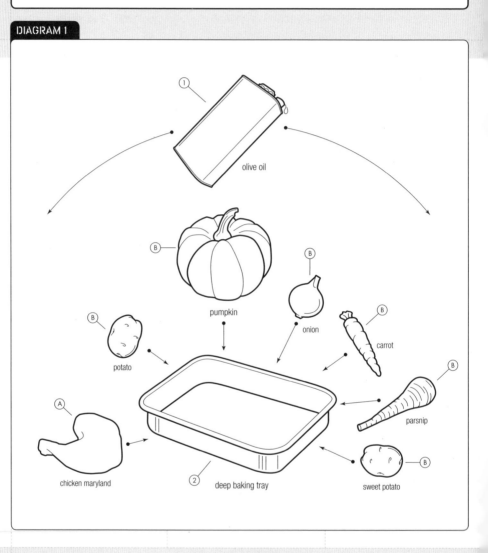

olive oil

pumpkin

onion

carrot

potato

parsnip

chicken maryland

deep baking tray

sweet potato

NOTES / MODS

74

PARTS:

(A) As many chicken Maryland pieces as you
    want (your chicken guy will know what this is)
(B) any or all of these (as many as you want):
    potato
    pumpkin
    onion
    carrot
    parsnip
    sweet potato

TOOLS:

(1) olive oil
(2) 1 deep baking tray

ASSEMBLY:

Set the oven at 180°C.

Peel your vegies and chop them up. Try and make
the bigger pieces roughly the same size.

Throw the chicken and the vegies in the baking
tray and give everything a good once over with
the olive oil.

Bang the tray in the oven and go and do something
else for 90 minutes.

If you remember, a poke and a prod won't go
astray midway through cooking.

SERVES: 1 Maryland per person

PREP TIME: 10 minutes. More if
you're having a lot of veg

COOK TIME: 90 minutes

*Add the seasoning of your choice
after you've oiled everything up.*

TIP / OPTION

[AFTERS

MARS BAR SLICE

This tasty treat requires you work quickly, but the hardest part is to not lick the spoon before you're done.

DIAGRAM 1

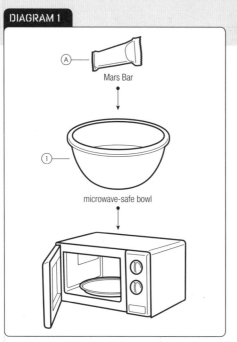

Ⓐ Mars Bar

① microwave-safe bowl

DIAGRAM 2

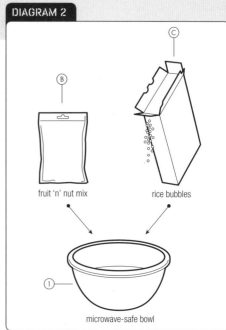

Ⓑ fruit 'n' nut mix

Ⓒ rice bubbles

① microwave-safe bowl

DIAGRAM 3

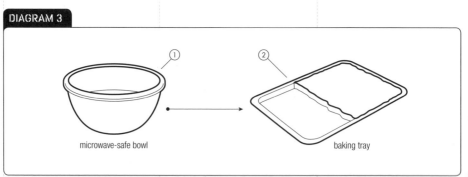

① microwave-safe bowl

② baking tray

NOTES / MODS

PARTS:

(A) 1 Mars Bar
(B) fruit 'n' nut mix
(C) ½ cup Rice Bubbles

TOOLS:

(1) 1 microwave-safe bowl
(2) 1 baking tray

ASSEMBLY:

Slice the Mars Bar into chunks and drop them into a microwave-safe bowl. Zap them on high for 10 seconds. Pull them out and stir them around a bit.

Don't lick the spoon.

Repeat this process another one or two times. You want the Mars Bar melted but not molten so shorten the microwave time for each repeat.

Quickly dump a handful or two of the fruit 'n' nut mix and the Rice Bubbles onto the melted Mars Bar and mix everything together.

Still working quickly, tip the contents of the dish onto the baking tray and pack everything down as best you can.

If you don't have enough mixture to fill the tray, just jam everything in one end.

Okay, now you can lick the spoon.

Put the tray in the fridge and let it set for 20 minutes or so. When it's cool, cut the slice into pieces and serve it up.

SERVES: As many people as you want to share it with

PREP TIME: If this takes longer than 5 minutes you're too slow

COOL TIME: About 20 minutes

TIP / OPTION

The temptation to snack on the Mars Bar before you finish making this dish is excruciating. Buy two Mars Bars and eat one while you're in the process of putting it together.

LOVE HANDLES

Make these if you've had a blue with the Missus. They'll bake themselves into a handle bar shape, but tell Her they're heart shaped and you're off the hook.

DIAGRAM 1

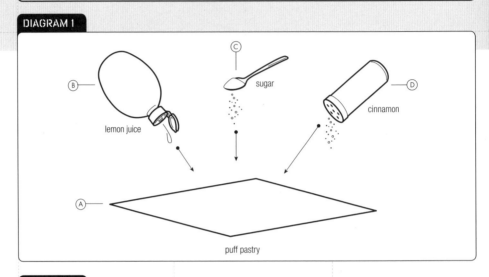

B — lemon juice
C — sugar
D — cinnamon
A — puff pastry

DIAGRAM 2

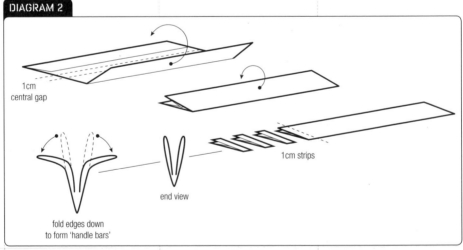

1cm central gap

fold edges down to form 'handle bars'

end view

1cm strips

NOTES / MODS

PARTS:

(A) 2 sheets puff pastry

(B) lemon juice

(C) lots of sugar

(D) lots of cinnamon

TOOLS:

(1) 1 baking tray

SERVES: Depends on how much trouble you are in. Make a double batch if you're really in deep

PREP TIME: 10 minutes

COOK TIME: 15 minutes

ASSEMBLY:

Squirt 1 side of the puff pastry sheet with a little lemon juice, using your hand to spread it over the surface.

Generously cover it with sugar and then with cinnamon. Press the sugar and cinnamon down into the pastry with your hands. Repeat for other side.

Fold the pastry edges in to the centre, leaving a 1 cm gap, and then fold the edges together again.

Cut into 1 cm strips and arrange as 'T's on the baking tray.

Repeat process for second sheet.

Bake for 15 minutes on 200°C, or until they start to look brown.

Allow to cool for a couple of minutes and then pile onto a plate. Sprinkle more sugar over the delicious golden mountain you have just made.

Serve while still warm. (They're still good cold, too.)

To save some space on the tray, stagger the positioning of the 'T's.

TIP / OPTION

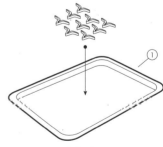

baking tray

Guaranteed. This dish will fill the hole in your stomach or bog up the rust holes in your car.

DIAGRAM 1

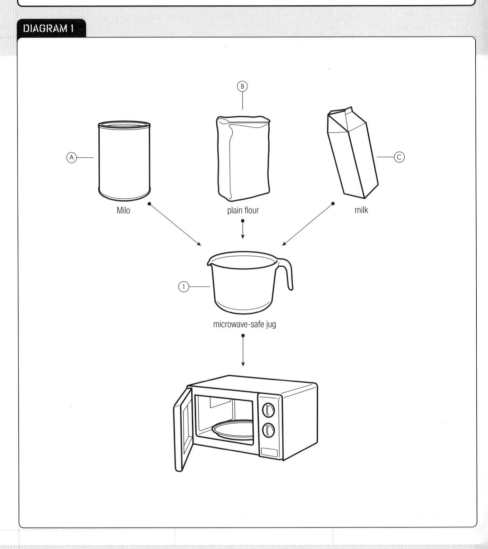

Milo

plain flour

milk

microwave-safe jug

NOTES / MODS

PARTS:

(A) 2 or 3 heaped teaspoons Milo

(B) 1 heaped teaspoon plain flour

(C) 1 cup milk

TOOLS:

(1) 1 microwave-safe jug

SERVES: Enough for 1 at a time

PREP TIME: 1 minute

COOK TIME: A couple of minutes

ASSEMBLY:

In a microwave-safe jug, mix together the Milo, flour and milk.

Microwave for 30 seconds and stir. Repeat this process until the mixture becomes thick enough to not fall off your spoon.

Keep an eye on this and a finger on the stop button through the heating stage. It'll go Vesuvius otherwise.

If you're not 'entertaining', eat it straight from the jug.

Add a large dollop of ice-cream to the other ingredients for a creamier mix.

TIP / OPTION

This is a dessert you can make for Her, but make sure you keep the stacks on the small side (they're so sweet you'll run the risk of sending Her into toxic shock). However, if you're making these for yourself, the sky's the limit.

DIAGRAM 1

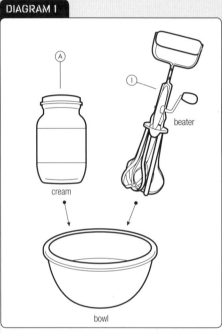

A
cream
① beater
bowl

DIAGRAM 2

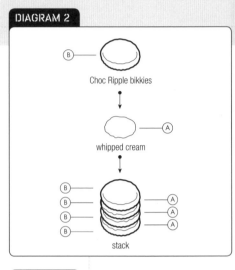

B
Choc Ripple bikkies
A
whipped cream
B B B B
A A A
stack

DIAGRAM 3

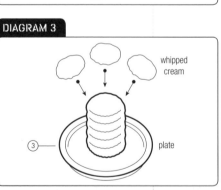

whipped cream
③ plate

DIAGRAM 4

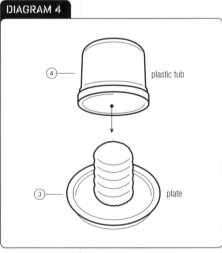

④ plastic tub
③ plate

NOTES / MODS

PARTS:

(A) 1 large tub cream (or as much as required)

(B) 1 pack Arnott's Choc Ripple bikkies
    (or as many as required)

TOOLS:

(1) 1 beater

(2) 1 bowl

(3) 1 small plate (per stack)

(4) 1 plastic tub

ASSEMBLY:

Whip the cream until it's thick enough to not fall off the beater.

Trowel it between 2 bikkies and keep doing so until you have a small stack. It's up to you how high you go.

When you're happy with the construction, trowel more cream over the stack until it's completely covered.

Cover it with a plastic tub and stick it in the fridge for a couple of hours so the bikkies soften up.

SERVES: As many as you want to make

PREP TIME: 15–20 minutes.
The stacks can get fiddly

COOL TIME: A couple of hours
– if you can wait that long

Grate some chocolate or crumble a chocolate bar (e.g. Flake) over your stacks.

Tip / Option

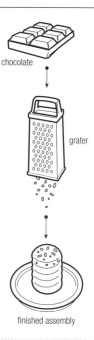

chocolate

grater

finished assembly

ICED COFFEE FRUIT CAKE

Make this cake and you've got smoko covered for weeks. Just wrap the cake in alfoil and keep it in the fridge. Tell your work mates your Mum came good with the chew and they'll think it tastes even better.

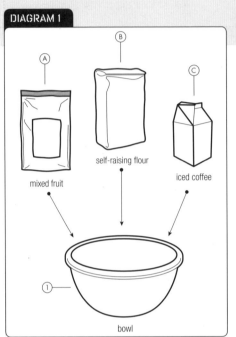

DIAGRAM 1

Ⓐ mixed fruit

Ⓑ self-raising flour

Ⓒ iced coffee

① bowl

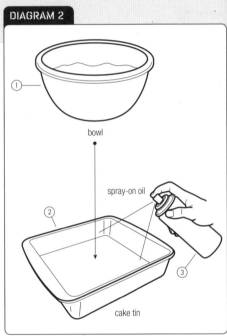

DIAGRAM 2

① bowl

② cake tin

③ spray-on oil

NOTES / MODS

76

PARTS:

(A) 500 g mixed fruit

(B) 2 cups self-raising flour

(C) 500 ml iced coffee

TOOLS:

(1) 1 bowl

(2) 1 cake tin

(3) something greasy (spray-on oil, olive oil,
     margarine, etc)

ASSEMBLY:

Whack all the ingredients into a bowl and give
it a good mix.

Grease up the cake tin and dump the mix into it.

Bake in the oven for 1 hour on 180°C. Test to see
if it's cooked by poking a fork into it. If the fork
comes out clean, tip the cake out and let it cool.

Slice it up and go for it.

SERVES: Heaps

PREP TIME: 10 minutes

COOK TIME: 1 hour

TIP / OPTION

*Use 500 ml of ANY liquid you
like. Try 500 ml of orange juice,
or mix 250 ml of Port with 250 ml
of water. If you're up for it, give
Coke a go.*

After dinner stuff yourself with a stuffed banana.

DIAGRAM 1

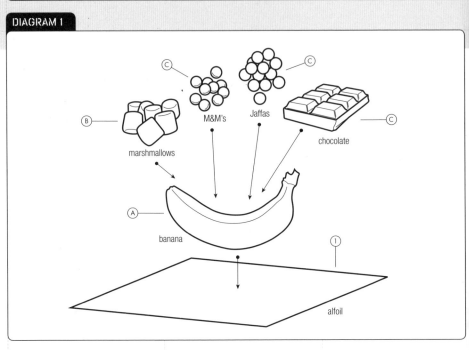

DIAGRAM 1

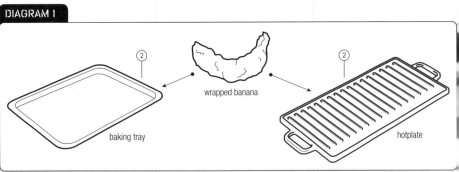

NOTES / MODS

PARTS:

(A) bananas

(B) marshmallows

(C) anything like M&Ms, Smarties, Jaffas or a
     broken-up chocolate bar.

TOOLS:

(1) alfoil

(2) 1 baking tray or hotplate

ASSEMBLY:

Grab a banana and pretend it's a hotdog bun.
Leave the peel on and cut down its length.
Be careful not to slice it in half.

Now, open the banana and fill it with your
goodies. Cut up the marshmallows if they're
too big to go in.

Close the banana as best you can, wrap it in the
alfoil and put on a baking tray. Place it in the oven
for about 5 minutes at 180°C or until the chocolate
melts.

SERVES: Start with 1 banana per
person

PREP TIME: Not long. Depends on
how much you want to jam in

COOK TIME: 5 minutes

*If you're BBQ-ing, whack some of
these on the grill for dessert.*

TIP / OPTION

If you like sweet things, this bad boy is for you. Keep this away from kids – they'll be pinging off the walls for days if they get hold of it.

DIAGRAM 1

A chocolate

① microwave-safe jug

B condensed milk

C crushed unsalted peanuts

① microwave-safe jug

② spray-on oil

③ baking tray

NOTES / MODS

PARTS:

(A) 1 150 g block of chocolate

(B) 200 g condensed milk

(C) crushed unsalted peanuts (optional)

TOOLS:

(1) 1 microwave-safe jug

(2) something greasy (spray-on oil, olive oil, margarine, etc)

(3) 1 baking tray

ASSEMBLY:

Break up the chockie bar into individual squares and throw them into a microwave-safe jug with the condensed milk.

Microwave on high for 1 minute or so until everything has melted.

If you're going to add nuts, now is the time to do it.

Give everything a good stir.

While it is still hot, pour the mixture into the greased baking tray. Stick it in the fridge to cool.

Once it has firmed, slice it up and go visit sugar Heaven.

SERVES: Lots and lots

PREP TIME: 3 minutes

COOK TIME: 1 minute

You might want to think about taking up a gym membership to work off the fudge.

TIP / OPTION

Take these lists with you when you go for supplies. Visit www.beatheateat.com and download and print these guys off, or photocopy and cut out the lists you need.

EMERGENCY CHIPS

PARTS:
bread (sliced)
1 packet French onion soup mix

NOAH'S MUFFINS

PARTS:
self-raising flour
grated cheese
2 eggs
milk

TOASTED EGGS

PARTS:
2 eggs

QWIK DIPS

TUNA DIP
PARTS:
150 g tub Philadelphia cream cheese
80 g can tuna in brine

CURRY DIP
PARTS:
300 ml plain yoghurt
Tikka Masala curry paste

CHEESY DIP CHEAT
PARTS:
Spreadable cheese (eg Kraft)

NUTS & BOLTS

PARTS:
Nutri-Grain cereal
unsalted peanuts
1 packet French onion soup mix

LEFTOVER SAUSAGE ROLLS

PARTS:
a bunch of left-over sausages
puff pastry

COKE CHICKEN

PARTS:
1 litre Coke
tomato sauce (optional)
4 chicken breasts
(or similar quantity of drumsticks
and/or wings)

CRUNCHY CHICKEN

PARTS:
1 bag potato chips
chicken pieces – as many as you
want

HALF TIME PIE

PARTS:
410 g can braised steak and onions
puff pastry

FAST FISH

PARTS:

a nice meaty piece of fish
(salmon, flake, tuna, etc)
lemon juice
salt and pepper (optional)

SOUPER PASTA

PARTS:

your choice of pasta
420 g can creamy mushroom soup
100 g pack of ham
4–5 mushrooms
yoghurt (optional)
cheese (optional)

STICKY CHICKEN

PARTS:

8 or so pieces of chicken
(drumsticks, wings or both)
soy sauce
honey
sweet chilli sauce
garlic (optional, but good to add)

CHARRED CHILLI CHICKEN

PARTS:

sweet chilli sauce
chicken breasts – as many as you
can eat

BEER CHICKEN

PARTS:

1 whole chicken
1 can beer of your choice

HOT TUNA WRAPS

PARTS:

couscous
425 g can tuna in springwater
375 g jar salsa
310 g can creamed corn
frozen peas
salt and pepper to taste
1 packet mountain bread
    (or similar flat bread)

EZ PIZZA BASE

PARTS: *Will make 1 thick
or 2 thin bases*
2 sachets instant yeast
salt
sugar
plain flour

EZ-ER PIZZA BASE

PARTS:

self-raising flour
200 ml plain yoghurt

SOUPER PORK

PARTS:

420 g can tomato soup
1 packet French onion soup mix
2 large or 4 small pork chops
rice

SUPPLIES

JOIN THE WILD FRONTIER
www.BeatHeatEat.com

CHILLI BEANS

PARTS:
1 medium onion
400 g can diced tomatoes
2 capsicums (1 red, 1 green)
420 g can baked beans
435 g can refried beans
375 g jar salsa
310 g can corn kernels (optional)
chilli flakes
tomato sauce
salt and pepper
cheese (optional)

3-2-1 RIBS

PARTS:
1 rack pork ribs
BBQ sauce

BOY BURGERS

PARTS:
1 onion
2 sachets beef-flavoured Cup o' Soup
400 g beef mince
tomato sauce
salt and pepper

MEATBALLS

PARTS:
400 g can tomato soup
sausages (flavour of your choice)
tomato sauce (optional)
420 g can spaghetti
400 g can diced tomatoes (optional)

PEANUT CHICKEN

PARTS:
1 onion
garlic (optional)
2 chicken breasts
crunchy peanut butter
honey
wholegrain mustard
curry powder

GIRL BURGERS

PARTS:
1 210 g can salmon
instant oats
1 egg
curry powder

BEEF & BROC

PARTS:
300 g beef strips
420 g can condensed tomato soup
tomato sauce
soy sauce
garlic (optional)
chilli flakes (optional)
broccoli

CHOP 'N' GO

PARTS:
chicken pieces (as many as you want)
any or all of these
(as many as you want):
potato, pumpkin, onion, carrot,
parsnip, sweet potato

MARS BAR SLICE

PARTS:
1 Mars Bar
fruit 'n' nut mix
Rice Bubbles

LOVE HANDLES

PARTS:
puff pastry
lemon juice
sugar
cinnamon

MILO MUD

PARTS:
Milo
plain flour
milk

CHOC RIPPLE STACKS

PARTS:
1 large tub cream
Arnott's Choc Ripple bikkies

ICED COFFEE FRUIT CAKE

PARTS:
500 g mixed fruit
self-raising flour
500 ml iced coffee

STUFFED BANANAS

PARTS:
bananas
marshmallows
anything like M&Ms, Smarties, Jaffas
or a broken-up chocolate bar.

FUDGED FUDGE

PARTS:
150 g block of chocolate
200 g condensed milk
crushed unsalted peanuts (optional)

SUPPLIES

AUTHOR BIO

I am a graphic designer who works from home in Adelaide, South Australia, with my wife Katharine and son Matthew.

Although this book makes it appear I have plenty of time on my hands, I really don't. I have designed heaps of book covers, well over a hundred by now, and numerous books for others which have been recognised by some, but not enough, of the right people.

So I figured I might as well make my day job a night one as well and have a crack at a book myself. They say you should write about something you know – and I know eating. It's the cooking part I have trouble with. That's why the recipes in here are so easy. If I can make them, anyone can.

This is the second book I have conceived, contructed and convinced Wakefield Press to publish, but the first I have written – with plenty of help, of course.

THANKS: Firstly to Katharine for her patience and understanding (read: letting me mess the kitchen and then fronting up for taste testing). F – for inspiration. You ARE the man. We'll get it next time. Mum, who continues to experiment with these recipes. Kathy for making everything 'even more thorough-est'. And, of course, Michael and Steph at Wakefield for coming back for seconds. Nice one, guys. What's next?